# *Mmm...* mushrooms

### VICTORIA LLOYD-DAVIES

### Foreword by ANTONIO CARLUCCIO

**SIMON & SCHUSTER**
**A VIACOM COMPANY**

First published in Great Britain by Simon & Schuster UK Ltd, 2000

A Viacom Company

1 3 5 7 9 10 8 6 4 2

Simon & Schuster UK Ltd

Africa House

64-78 Kingsway

London WC2B 6AH

Design: Jane Humphrey

Typesetting: Stylize Digital Artwork

Photographer: Simon Smith

Home economist: Wendy Dines

Stylist: Penny Markham

Nutritionist: Jane Griffin

Printed and bound in: Hong Kong, Singapore, Italy, Great Britain

A CIP catalogue record for this book is available from the British Library

ISBN 0-85941-984-3

Ⓥ shows the recipe is suitable for vegetarians

ⓋⒼ shows the recipe is suitable for vegans

contents

# mushrooms

foreword by Antonio Carluccio

Following on from the huge success of her first mushroom cookbook, Victoria Lloyd-Davies has written a second book, once again full of delicious, creative and inspiring mushroom recipes which show just how versatile the mushroom is. Since the cultivation of button mushrooms was first developed 350 years ago, progress in the science of agriculture has meant that many more varieties can be cultivated today. We seem to have learned many of the secrets of the wilderness and by means of controlled environments we can make the traditional closed and open white mushrooms readily available all year round. Through various new techniques, brown caps, oyster, shiitake, horse, blewit and enoki mushrooms are now cultivated. The wide variety of cultivated mushrooms now available, with their different colours, sizes, shapes and textures make cooking with mushrooms a real adventure and Victoria has certainly made the most of them in these delicious, enticing recipes.

Vegetarians, especially, will enjoy cooking with mushrooms since they don't require a lot of preparation and create a wide variety of sophisticated dishes. Equally, the non-vegetarian will find endless inspiration on these pages.

As a wild mushroom fanatic, I must say that I am a little jealous about what Victoria has achieved with the cultivated variety. Her recipes are imaginative, easy to prepare and above all, very tasty, tempting everyone to cook them. In her work Victoria demonstrates that with conviction and passion you can turn a humble cultivated mushroom into superb food.

I would not hesitate to recommend this book to anybody interested in exploring and savouring the many exciting flavours of fungi.

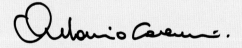

## Introduction

The Pharaohs of Ancient Egypt called them "the food from heaven" and since they were first cultivated in France in 1650, the number of cultivated mushroom varieties has increased significantly due to their popularity. In Britain we started to grow them seriously in the 1940s. Now they are the most valuable horticultural crop sold in this country. And not only are they delicious and versatile, they are also extremely good for us since they are low in salt and fat and cholesterol-free.

## Cultivation

Mushrooms grow in the dark but the growers do turn the lights on to pick them! They are grown on pasteurised compost in conditions which aim to imitate the ideal conditions in nature as closely as possible. The best climate for mushrooms is created by damp autumn mornings. In order to grow mushrooms so that mushrooms are available all year round, the mushroom grower recreates this climate by using air-cooling in the summer and heating in the winter. Mushroom growers use health-conscious growing methods and grow mushrooms naturally; this normally takes about six weeks and then the mushrooms are picked by hand. Mushrooms are one of the freshest vegetables in our shops since they tend to be on the supermarket shelf a mere twenty-four hours after being picked.

The *White* mushroom (see photographs below), which accounts for the majority of mushroom sales, is picked at four different stages (grades) in its growing cycle which produces the following four types of mushrooms:
*Button mushrooms (1st stage);*
*Closed Cup mushrooms (2nd stage);*
*Open Cup mushrooms (3rd stage);*
*Large Flat mushrooms (4th stage).*

A *Button* mushroom (Agaricus bisporus), if not picked, will double in size every twenty-four hours. First, it develops into a *Closed Cup* mushroom and then grows to become an *Open Cup* mushroom with the brown gills visible underneath. This mushroom will grow further to become a *Large Flat* mushroom; it takes five days for each tiny *Button* mushroom to grow into a very *Large Flat* mushroom. As a mushroom increases in size and maturity, so its flavour develops and improves. By far the most popular mushroom is the *Closed Cup* mushroom, which is a wonderfully versatile and delicious vegetable that can be used in so many ways.

## Cultivated Exotic Mushrooms

An increasing number of cultivated exotic or speciality mushrooms is now available in Britain. Mushroom growers travel the world learning about new types of mushrooms and are now able to cultivate more wild species than ever and extend the typically short growing season.

*Brown* mushrooms (Agaricus bisporus *syn. A. brunnescens*) are also called *Brown Cap, Chestnut, Champignon Marron* or *Portabello* mushrooms. These mushrooms have a firmer

*Button mushrooms*
*(1st stage)*

*Closed Cup mushrooms*
*(2nd stage)*

*Open Cup mushrooms*
*(3rd stage)*

*Large Flat mushrooms*
*(4th stage)*

*Brown mushrooms*

*Oyster mushrooms*

*Shiitake mushrooms*

thoroughly to bring out their unique, fragrant taste. They taste delicious fried with bacon or cooked in creamy sauces, casseroles and risottos.

texture and a stronger, nuttier flavour than white mushrooms. They are sold in two sizes. The smaller ones are called *Brown Cap*, *Chestnut*, *Crimini* or *Portabellini* mushrooms. The larger ones, with the gills showing underneath, are called *Flat Chestnut* or *Portabello* mushrooms.

*Oyster* mushrooms are either grey (Pleurotus ostreatus), brown (Pleurotus pulmonarius), pink (Pleurotus djamor) or yellow (Pleurotus citrinopileatus). These delicate mushrooms need very little cooking. They are delicious in light creamy sauces, risottos and omelettes.

*Shiitake* mushrooms (Lentinus edodes) are the direct opposite of white mushrooms in appearance – they have dark brown caps and white gills instead of white caps and brown gills. Trim off the stalks, as they can be tough. Shiitake mushrooms have a unique chewy texture and subtle flavour. When cooked in rich sherry or wine sauces, they are ideal partners for game and red meat. They are also good in Japanese dishes.

Some of the newer and more unusual cultivated exotic mushrooms are listed below:

*Blewit* mushrooms (Lepista nuda) have blue-tinted stalks and white caps. Some people may be sensitive to blewits eaten raw. It is recommended that these mushrooms are sliced and cooked

*Enoki* mushrooms (Flammulina velutipes) are crisp white mushrooms with long thin stems and tiny white caps. They are best eaten raw in salads or tossed into stir-fries at the last minute.

*Hon-shimeji* mushrooms (Hypsizygus tessulatus) are sold in clusters. Each mushroom on the cluster is very small with a dark cap and light gills. Gently break up the cluster to cook them but do not discard the stalks. These zesty mushrooms, with a crisp texture, are excellent sautéed in butter and served as a vegetable. They are used extensively in Japanese dishes.

*Horse* mushrooms (Agaricus arvensis) have long stems and either white or pale yellow caps. These mushrooms have a distinctive aniseed fragrance and subtle flavour. Their texture is similar to the white mushroom so they can be used in any white mushroom recipe.

**Buying Mushrooms**
At a time when we are all being encouraged to eat more vegetables, the healthy mushroom comes into its own.

*Horse mushrooms*

*Blewit mushrooms*

*Enoki mushrooms*

Mushrooms are easy to prepare and are wonderful in a wide variety of dishes ranging from cool summer salads to hot winter casseroles. Handle them with care as they bruise easily. Once purchased, put them in their paper bag in the salad drawer of the refrigerator and consume them within three days. If you buy them pre-packaged, take off the cling film and slip the mushrooms into a paper bag or wrap them in absorbent kitchen paper.

### Preparation

Rinse mushrooms quickly under cold running water and dry them on absorbent kitchen paper just before you use them. Never peel cultivated mushrooms and only trim off their stalks if they are tough. The whole mushroom is edible and the skin is not only flavourful but nutritious so nothing needs to be wasted when cooking with mushrooms.

### Freezing

Fresh mushrooms are in good supply all year. However, if you find a bargain, why not make some mushroom soup (see page 8) or ketchup (see page 78) and some concentrated mushroom purée to use in sauces or stir-fries. For each pound of fresh mushrooms, allow four shallots and 10g (½oz) fresh parsley. Chop everything very finely, preferably in a food processor. Melt 50g (2oz) butter in a large pan, add the mushroom mixture and cook over a moderate heat, stirring frequently, for about 10 minutes or until all the liquid has evaporated and the mixture is dry and glossy. Cool, and then freeze in an ice cube tray covered with foil. Add four cubes of this mushroom mixture to each pint of liquid.

### Mushrooms Contribute to Good Health

Mushrooms are an ideal food – they contain only negligible amounts of fat, sugar and salt and are cholesterol free. They are a valuable source of dietary fibre which, among other things, will help to satisfy hungry slimmers. Mushrooms are very flavourful and so they are ideal for low-salt diets which may help to reduce the incidence of heart disease, high blood pressure and stroke.

Mushrooms are a good source of B vitamins – niacin, riboflavin, thiamine, folic acid and pantothenic acid. These vitamins are often lost when vegetables are cooked in boiling water but since mushrooms are seldom boiled, the B vitamins are retained. These vitamins may help to relieve stress, depression and fatigue, and give you strong and healthy hair, skin and nails. Mushrooms are also one of the few dietary sources of vitamin D.

Mushrooms are a good source of minerals, especially potassium which is essential to balance the sodium found in other foods, phosphorus and selenium

Mushrooms are a good source of easily absorbed, high quality protein, and contain more than most other vegetables.

*Kcal and fat content are per serving unless otherwise stated.*

### Nutrition
*Food Value per 100g*

| | |
|---|---|
| Energy | 13 kcals (55kJ) |
| Protein | 1.8g |
| Carbohydrate | 0.4g |
| (of which sugars) | 0.2g |
| (of which starch) | 0.2g |
| Fat | 0.5g |
| (of which saturates) | 0.1g |
| Fibre | 2.3g |
| Sodium | 5.0mg |

**170**kcals

**13**g fat

450ml (16 fl oz) hot vegetable stock

175g (6oz) potato, scrubbed and cut into small dice

575g (1¼lb) open cup mushrooms, chopped roughly

2 tablespoons tapenade

4 tablespoons crème fraîche

salt and freshly ground black pepper

## Speedy Mushroom Soup

*Preparation and cooking time: 20 minutes · Serves 4*

Pour the stock into a large saucepan. Add the diced potato, mushrooms and tapenade. Cover and bring to the boil. Simmer for 10 minutes. Blend in a food processor until fairly smooth. Season to taste. Return to the heat and gently stir in the crème fraîche.

**170**kcals

**15**g fat

450g (1lb) small closed cup mushrooms

450ml (16 fl oz) hot vegetable stock

grated rind and juice of 1 lime

3 tablespoons chopped fresh mint

3 tablespoons sherry

284ml carton of single cream

salt and freshly ground black pepper

**To garnish:**

single cream

button mushrooms, sliced

sprigs of fresh mint, shredded

## Special Mushroom Soup

*Preparation and cooking time: 10 minutes · Serves 4*

Put the mushrooms, stock, grated rind and juice of lime, mint and sherry into a saucepan. Bring to the boil and simmer for 3 minutes. Blend in a food processor until fairly smooth. Return to the pan, stir in the cream and reheat gently, but do not allow to boil. Season to taste, then serve garnished with a swirl of cream, sliced mushrooms and shredded mint.

starters

*Special Mushroom Soup*

## Roasted Mushrooms and Onions in Filo Tartlets

*Preparation time: 20 minutes · Cooking time: 35 minutes · Serves 4*

Preheat the oven to Gas 6/400°F/200°C. Lay one sheet of filo pastry on the work surface and brush with egg white. Fold in half, then brush the top with egg white. Fold in half again to give a rectangle approximately 20 × 15cm (8 × 6 inches). Use to line the base and sides of a 10cm (4-inch) round loose-bottomed fluted flan tin, pressing the pastry into the flutes. Trim the excess pastry. Repeat with the remaining filo pastry to line three more flan tins. Bake in the oven for about 8 minutes. Remove from the flan tins, carefully brush the outside with egg white, then return to oven, upside down on a baking sheet for 5 minutes, until golden brown.

      Put the onion wedges in a roasting tin, and then drizzle over the oil. Roast in the oven for 10–15 minutes. Stir in the red pesto and mushrooms. Season to taste. Return to the oven for 8–10 minutes. Spoon the mixture into the warm filo pastry cases. Drizzle with lime juice.

4 sheets of filo pastry
1 large egg white, lightly beaten
**For the filling:**
3 × 75g (3oz) red onions, each cut into
    12 wedges
1 tablespoon olive oil
4 tablespoons red pesto
2 × 125g packs of oyster mushrooms, torn
juice of 1 lime
salt and freshly ground black pepper

**175** kcals

**10** g fat

## Chilled Mushrooms in Curry Sauce

*Preparation time: 10 minutes + 2 hours chilling · Serves 6*

Mix the ingredients for the curry sauce together. Chill for about 2 hours. Stir in the mushrooms and almonds. Arrange the salad leaves on individual plates and spoon the mushroom and curry mixture on to the side. Garnish with coriander.

350g (12oz) closed cup mushrooms, halved
50g (2oz) blanched almonds, toasted
200g pack of washed and ready-to-eat
    continental four leaf salad
**For the curry sauce:**
200g carton of fromage frais
2 teaspoons curry paste
2 tablespoons mango chutney
2 tablespoons fresh lime juice
chopped coriander, to garnish

**110** kcals

**5** g fat

Ⓥ

Tip: The next time you make scrambled eggs, try
adding some cooked mushrooms and serve them together on toast.

*Roasted Mushrooms and Onions in Filo Tartlets*

**75** kcals

**5** g fat

(VG)

120g pack of shiitake mushrooms, stalks
   trimmed
125g pack of oyster mushrooms
225g (8oz) brown/chestnut mushrooms,
   sliced thinly
2 tablespoons olive oil
2 garlic cloves, chopped finely
4 tablespoons rosé wine
40g pack of lambs lettuce
extra-virgin olive oil, to garnish
salt and freshly ground black pepper

## Exotic Mushrooms in Garlic and Rosé Wine

*Preparation and cooking time: 20 minutes · Serves 4*

Halve any large shiitake and oyster mushrooms. Heat the oil. Add the
garlic and shiitake mushrooms and cook in a covered pan over a medium
heat for 1 minute. Stir in the oyster and brown/chestnut mushrooms along
with the wine and cook for another minute. Allow to cool. Season to taste.
Gently stir in the lambs lettuce and spoon on to plates, ready to serve.
Drizzle over some extra-virgin olive oil. Enjoy the rest of the rosé wine
with your meal!

**220** kcals

**20** g fat

(VG)

450g (1lb) closed cup mushrooms, quartered
1 large red pepper, de-seeded and chopped
   very finely
1 tablespoon chopped fresh flat-leaf parsley
1 large ripe avocado, peeled and sliced
wedges of lime, to serve
**For the marinade:**
grated rind of 1 lime
juice of 2 limes
4 tablespoons olive oil
2 fresh chillies, de-seeded and chopped
   very finely
salt and freshly ground black pepper

## Mexican Mushrooms

*Preparation time: 2 hours marinating + 15 minutes · Serves 4*

Whisk the marinade ingredients together and then pour over the
mushrooms. Stir gently until all the mushrooms are well coated. Cover
and leave to marinate for 2 hours. Then stir in the red pepper and chopped
parsley. Season to taste. Arrange slices of avocado on four plates. Spoon
mushrooms to one side. Serve with wedges of lime.

Tip: Look out for packs of ready-sliced mushrooms for stir-fries and salads,
mushrooms with sauces, mushrooms with garlic butter –
all designed to make your life easier.

*Exotic Mushrooms in Garlic and Rosé Wine*

## Japanese-style Mushroom and Fish Plate

*Preparation time: 15 minutes + 6 hours chilling · Serves 4*

Skin the kipper fillets, then slice them into thin slivers. Place in a large shallow dish and scatter over the mushroom slices. Mix together the oil, orange juice, five-spice seasoning and dill. Pour the mixture over the mushrooms and fish making sure they are all well coated. Cover and chill for at least 6 hours, preferably overnight. Stir orange segments into the marinated fish and mushrooms. Serve garnished with fresh dill.

2 boneless kipper fillets (about 175g/6oz each)
200g pack of button mushrooms, sliced thickly
6 tablespoons walnut oil
juice of 1 medium-sized orange
½ teaspoon Chinese five-spice seasoning
2 tablespoons chopped fresh dill
2 large oranges, segmented
sprigs of fresh dill, to garnish

**415** kcals
**30** g fat

## Mushrooms à la grecque

*Preparation and cooking time: 20 minutes + 2 hours chilling · Serves 4*

Put all the ingredients for the marinade into a large saucepan. Cover and bring to the boil, then simmer for 5 minutes. Add the mushrooms, tomatoes and olives. Stir well. Cover the pan and simmer for 3 minutes. Remove the mushrooms to a serving bowl, and then boil the cooking liquor rapidly until reduced by half. Cool, discard the bay leaves, season to taste and then pour over the mushrooms. Chill for 2 hours before serving. Serve with pitta bread strips.

2 × 200g packs of baby button mushrooms
225g (8oz) vine-ripened tomatoes, peeled
    and chopped
12 black olives, stoned and chopped
salt and freshly ground black pepper
**For the marinade:**
5 tablespoons olive oil
150ml (¼ pint) dry white wine
1 garlic clove, crushed
2 fresh bay leaves
1 teaspoon coriander seeds, crushed lightly
2 pitta breads, warmed and cut into strips,
    to serve

**180** kcals
**15** g fat
(VG)

Tip: Mushrooms should be cooked and sautéed quickly
to retain their natural flavour and delicious texture.

*Mushrooms à la grecque*

**210** kcals

**15** g fat

V

2 × 125g packs of oyster mushrooms
1 litre (1¾ pints) oil, for frying
**For the batter:**
1 large egg yolk
100g (3½oz) cornflour
100ml (3½fl oz) cold water
a pinch of salt
**To serve:**
lemon wedges
brown bread and butter

## Mushrooms Tempura

*Preparation and cooking time: 15 minutes · Serves 4*

Tear the larger mushrooms into 1cm (½-inch) long strips. Heat the oil in a wok or deep frying pan. Mix all the ingredients for the batter together roughly, leaving some lumps of cornflour. Dip the mushrooms in the batter, then deep-fry in batches in the hot oil for 15 seconds. Drain on kitchen paper. Serve with lemon wedges and brown bread and butter.

**260** kcals

**25** g fat

V

16 even-sized open cup mushrooms, stalks
   cut level
3 tablespoons corn oil
75g (3oz) unsalted butter, softened
3 garlic cloves, chopped very finely
2 tablespoons chopped fresh thyme, stalks
   removed
1½ tablespoons lemon juice
50g (2oz) fresh breadcrumbs

## Roasted Garlic Mushrooms

*Preparation and cooking time: 20 minutes · Serves 4*

If you are entertaining, you can prepare this dish earlier in the day. Simply store in the refrigerator and cook in the oven when required. Allow four mushrooms per person. Preheat the oven to Gas 6/200°C/400°F. Lightly fry the mushrooms, cap-side down, in hot oil for twenty seconds, then arrange them in a shallow roasting tin with the stalks facing upwards. Mix together the butter, garlic, herbs, lemon juice and seasoning. Spoon a little garlic butter on to each mushroom, and then lightly press the breadcrumbs on top. Cook in the oven for 10 minutes.

*Mushrooms Tempura (top), Roasted Garlic Mushrooms*

## Mushroom Brunch

*Preparation and cooking time: 10 minutes · Serves 4*

Brush the mushroom caps lightly with oil and grill the mushrooms and bacon for 3 minutes. Turn the mushrooms and bacon over and grill for another 2 minutes. Meanwhile, toast the cut sides of the rolls. Place the mushrooms on one half of each roll. Spoon a little crème fraîche on to each mushroom, then top with bacon and mozzarella. Return to the grill and cook until the cheese has melted. Top with the remaining halves of roll.

4 large flat mushrooms
1 tablespoon oil
4 rashers of unsmoked bacon
4 ciabatta rolls, halved
2 tablespoons crème fraîche
75g (3oz) grated mozzarella cheese

**360** kcals

**15** g fat

brunches & light lunches

*Mushroom Brunch*

**1865** kcals
loaf

**80** g fat
loaf

225g (8oz) granary malted brown bread flour
125g (4½oz) strong white bread flour
1 teaspoon salt
1 sachet (6g) easy-blend dried yeast
225g (8oz) brown/chestnut mushrooms,
    chopped very finely
5 tablespoons olive oil
150ml (¼ pint) warm water
½ tsp sunflower oil, for greasing

## Rustic Mushroom Bread

*Preparation time: 15 minutes + 30 minutes – 1 hour rising time*
*Cooking time: 30–35 minutes · Makes 1 loaf*

Put all the ingredients except the sunflower oil in a large bowl and mix together to form a dough. Use the sunflower oil to grease a baking sheet. Knead on a lightly floured surface for five minutes. Roll into a 30 × 7.5cm (12 × 3-inch) sausage shape. Place on the oiled baking sheet. Make deep slashes at intervals in the dough. Cover with cling film and leave in a warm place until double in size. Preheat the oven to Gas 7/220°C/425°F. Remove the cling film. Dust the top of the bread with flour, then bake in the oven for 30–35 minutes.

**220** kcals

**20** g fat

75g (3oz) butter
4 garlic cloves, chopped very finely
grated rind of 1 lemon
450g (1lb) open cup mushrooms,
    chopped roughly
3 tablespoons chopped fresh parsley
4 tablespoons fresh soured cream
freshly ground black pepper

## Garlic Mushroom Pâté

*Preparation time: 10 minutes + 2 hours chilling · Serves 4*

Melt the butter in a large saucepan and add the garlic, lemon rind and mushrooms. Sauté over a high heat for about 2 minutes, stirring continuously. Turn into a food processor with the pepper and parsley. Blend for 30 seconds. Turn into a bowl and leave to cool. Stir in the soured cream and chill for at least 2 hours.

**275** kcals

**20** g fat

1 tablespoon sunflower oil
50g (2oz) butter
350g (12oz) closed cup mushrooms, quartered
125g pack of oyster mushrooms, torn
120g pack of shiitake mushrooms, halved
2 garlic cloves, chopped
2 tablespoons chopped fresh parsley
2 tablespoons crème fraîche
1 tablespoon Worcestershire sauce
50g (2oz) soft cheese with garlic and herbs
8 slices of toasted ciabatta bread (or other
    bread as preferred)
a sprig of parsley, to garnish

## Creamy Mushrooms on Ciabatta Toasts

*Preparation and cooking time: 10 minutes · Serves 4*

Heat the oil and butter in a large frying pan. Add all the mushrooms and the garlic and cook for 3 minutes, stirring frequently. Add the parsley, then stir in the crème fraîche and Worcestershire sauce. Cook for a further minute. Finally crumble in the cheese and stir until almost melted. Serve on the toasts. Garnish with parsley.

brunches & light lunches

20

*Creamy Mushrooms on Ciabatta Toasts*

## Mushroom Flan

*Preparation time: 15 minutes · Cooking time: 45 minutes · Serves 4*

Preheat the oven to Gas 6/200°C/400°F. To make the pastry, sift the flour into a bowl. Add the butter or margarine and then rub it in with the fingertips until the mixture resembles fine breadcrumbs. Add 2 tablespoons of cold water and fork through to make a firm dough. Roll out and use to line a 20cm (8-inch) flan dish. Prick the base with a fork. Line with greaseproof paper and fill with dried peas. Bake in the oven for 15 minutes.

Remove from the oven. Take off the peas and greaseproof paper. Reduce the oven temperature to Gas 5/190°C/375°F. Meanwhile, heat the oil in a pan and fry the onion gently for 2 minutes. Add the mushrooms and continue to cook for 5 minutes. Scatter the mushrooms, onions, cheese and thyme over the base of the cooked flan case. Beat together the eggs, seasoning and cream and pour over the mushrooms. Return to the oven and cook for a further 30 minutes. Serve warm or cold.

**560** kcals

**40** g fat

V

**For the pastry:**
150g (5½oz) plain flour
70g (2½oz) butter, cut into small pieces,
    or hard margarine

**For the filling:**
1 tablespoon olive oil
1 onion, chopped finely
225g (8oz) closed cup mushrooms, sliced
50g (2oz) Cheddar cheese, grated
1 tablespoon chopped fresh thyme
2 medium eggs, beaten
142ml carton of double cream
salt and freshly ground black pepper

## Mushroom with Herbs Soufflé Omelette

*Preparation time: 15 minutes · Cooking time: 20 minutes · Serves 4*

Put the filling ingredients into a pan. Cover and cook over a low heat for about 5 minutes. Whisk together the egg yolks and seasoning in a large bowl. Whisk the egg whites in a separate bowl until soft peaks form and then fold them into the egg yolks. Pre-heat the grill. Heat a teaspoon of oil in an omelette pan. Add a quarter of the egg mixture and cook for a few minutes until the base is firm. Then cook under the grill for 2 minutes to cook the top of the omelette. Transfer the omelette to a warm plate, spoon a quarter of the mushroom mixture over one half of the omelette, then flip over the other half. Serve immediately. Repeat three times to make four omelettes in total.

**290** kcals

**25** g fat

V

8 large eggs, separated
4 teaspoons olive oil
salt and freshly ground black pepper

**For the filling:**
225g (8oz) closed cup mushrooms, sliced
2 tablespoons snipped fresh chives
3 tablespoons coriander, chopped roughly
200ml carton of half-fat crème fraîche

*Mushroom Flan*

**For the pastry:**
150g (5½oz) plain flour
70g (2½oz) butter, cut into small pieces
1 tablespoon French peppercorn mustard
**For the filling:**
2 tablespoons olive oil
1 red onion, chopped finely
2 garlic cloves, chopped
450g (1lb) large flat mushrooms, sliced thickly
175g (6oz) mozzarella cheese, grated
2 tablespoons chopped fresh tarragon
2 tablespoons chives, snipped
salt and freshly ground black pepper

## Mushroom Tart

*Preparation time: 20 minutes + chilling · Cooking time: 20 minutes · Serves 4*
To make the pastry, sift the flour into a bowl and add the butter. Rub in with the fingertips until the mixture resembles fine breadcrumbs. Add 2 tablespoons of cold water and fork through to make a firm dough. Roll out and use to line a 24cm (9-inch) flan tin. Chill.

Preheat the oven to Gas 6/200°C/400°F. Heat the oil and cook the onion and garlic until soft. Then add the mushrooms and cook quickly for 5 minutes until all the liquid has evaporated. Spread the mustard over the base of the flan. Mix together the cheese, herbs and seasoning and then spoon half the mixture into the pastry case. Arrange the mushrooms on top and sprinkle over the remaining cheese. Bake in the oven at for 20 minutes until the cheese has turned golden brown.

355 kcals

30 g fat

curly leaf lettuce, torn into small pieces
2 celery sticks, chopped
celery leaves
225g (8oz) mature Cheddar cheese, broken
    into small chunks
350g (12oz) closed cup mushrooms,
    sliced thickly
8 pickled onions, halved
**For the dressing:**
4 tablespoons extra-virgin olive oil
2 tablespoons garlic wine vinegar
**To serve:**
crusty bread
spiced fruit chutney

## Ploughman's Lunch

*Preparation time: 15 minutes · Serves 4*
Whisk together the ingredients for the dressing. Put the remaining ingredients into a large salad bowl and pour over the dressing. Toss together. Serve the salad with slices of crusty bread and spiced fruit chutney.

Tip: The flavour of sautéed mushrooms is quite concentrated and they are therefore wonderful served cold as part of a sandwich filling. Sautéed mushrooms also freeze well and can be used later in cooked dishes.

*Ploughman's Lunch*

## Mixed Mushroom Risotto

*Preparation time: 10 minutes · Cooking time: 25 minutes · Serves 4*

Heat the oil and cook the onion and garlic for 3 minutes. Add the mushrooms and cook for 2 minutes. Stir in the rice and cook for a further minute. Pour in the wine and cook, stirring, until almost all the liquid has been absorbed. Stir in half the stock and cook gently, again stirring until almost all the liquid has been absorbed. Repeat with the remaining stock, season to taste and finally stir in the chopped fresh oregano. Serve topped with slivers of Parmesan cheese, if desired.

2 tablespoons olive oil
1 large red onion, chopped
2 garlic cloves, chopped finely
225g (8oz) brown/chestnut mushrooms, halved
125g pack of blewit mushrooms, quartered
125g pack of oyster mushrooms
120g pack of shiitake mushrooms
250g (9oz) risotto rice
150ml (¼ pint) white wine
750ml (1¼ pint) hot vegetable stock
2 tablespoons chopped fresh oregano
slivers of Parmesan cheese, to serve (optional)
salt and freshly ground black pepper

**355** kcals

**5** g fat

(V)

## Mushroom Goulash

*Preparation time: 10 minutes · Cooking time: 20 minutes · Serves 4*

Heat the oil and gently cook the leek and green pepper for 2 minutes. Stir in the mushrooms. Cover and cook gently for 5 minutes, stirring occasionally. Stir in the paprika pepper and cook for 1 minute. Add the stock, passata and parsley. Season to taste. Cook, uncovered, for 10 minutes, stirring occasionally. Meanwhile, cook the tagliatelle according to the pack instructions. Drain the tagliatelle and divide between four plates. Just before serving, stir the soured cream into the goulash and heat through. Serve with the tagliatelle.

2 tablespoons oil
1 large leek, sliced
1 green pepper, de-seeded and cut into
    small cubes
450g (1lb) closed cup mushrooms,
    sliced thickly
175g (6oz) brown/chestnut mushrooms,
    halved
2 tablespoons paprika pepper
150ml (¼ pint) vegetable stock
3 tablespoons passata
2 tablespoons chopped fresh parsley
2 tablespoons fresh soured cream
500g pack of fresh tagliatelle
salt and freshly ground black pepper

**115** kcals

**10** g fat

(V)

vegetarian meals

*Mixed Mushroom Risotto (top), Mushroom Goulash*

**590** kcals

**35** g fat

(V)

25g (1oz) butter
1 onion, chopped very finely
450g (1lb) closed cup mushrooms, sliced
2 tablespoons chopped fresh marjoram
¼ teaspoon cayenne pepper
10 sheets ready-to-use egg lasagne
**For the cheese sauce:**
50g (2oz) butter
50g (2oz) plain flour
600ml (1 pint) milk
225g (8oz) mozzarella cheese, grated
1 medium egg, beaten

## Mushroom Lasagne

*Preparation time: 20 minutes · Cooking time: 40 minutes + 5 minutes standing · Serves 4*

To make the cheese sauce, put the butter, flour and milk into a saucepan. Heat slowly, whisking continuously, until the butter has melted. Then bring to the boil, stirring, until the sauce has thickened. Take off the heat and stir in three quarters of the cheese and the beaten egg. Cover the pan until required. Preheat the oven to Gas 4/180°C/350°F. Melt the butter and cook the onion and mushrooms for 5 minutes. Stir in the marjoram.

Spoon a little cheese sauce into the base of an oiled, shallow ovenproof dish. Place a layer of lasagne sheets on the sauce, and then spoon on some of the mushroom mixture. Repeat the layers, ending with the cheese sauce on top. Sprinkle over the remaining cheese and cayenne pepper. Cover with lightly greased foil and cook in the oven for 20 minutes. Remove the foil and continue to cook for a further 20 minutes. Allow to stand for 5 minutes before serving.

**595** kcals

**40** g fat

(V)

250g (9oz) brown rice
2 tablespoons olive oil
a bunch of spring onions, chopped
2 garlic cloves, crushed
175g (6oz) large flat mushrooms, sliced
125g pack of blewit mushrooms, sliced
200g pack of horse mushrooms, halved
120g pack of shiitake mushrooms
1 tablespoon paprika pepper
4 tablespoons chopped fresh parsley
300g carton of crème fraîche

## Mixed Mushroom Stroganoff

*Preparation time: 15 minutes · Cooking time: 15 minutes · Serves 4*

Cook the rice according to the pack instructions. Meanwhile, heat the oil in a large saucepan and cook the spring onions and garlic for 2 minutes. Stir in all the mushrooms. Cover and cook over a gentle heat for 8 to 10 minutes, stirring occasionally. Add the paprika pepper and parsley. Stir in the crème fraîche and heat through gently for about 4 minutes. Serve with the cooked rice.

*Mixed Mushroom Stroganoff*

## Mushroom Strudels

*Preparation time: 25 minutes · Cooking time: 30 minutes · Serves 4*

Preheat the oven to Gas 4/180°C/350°F. Heat the oil in a pan and cook the celery and red pepper for 2 minutes. Drain and cool. Put the diced apple into a bowl with the lemon juice to stop the apple from going brown. Mix the mushrooms, cheese and basil together in another bowl. Lift the apple out of the lemon juice and drain. Stir the apple into the mushroom mixture with the cooled celery and red pepper. Brush a sheet of filo pastry with melted butter, then fold in half to give a rectangle 23 × 28cm (9 × 11 inches). Brush the top of the pastry with more butter, and then sprinkle some breadcrumbs over the top. Place a quarter of the mushroom mixture two-thirds of the way down the pastry. Starting at the shorter edge and at the end where the mushroom mixture is, carefully roll up the pastry to form a sausage shape. Place on a lightly greased baking sheet. Repeat with the remaining pastry and mushroom mixture to make four strudels. Brush the strudels with the melted butter and sprinkle the remaining breadcrumbs over the top. Bake in the oven for 30 minutes.

**515** kcals

**30** g fat

Ⓥ

2 teaspoons oil
1 celery stick, chopped very finely
½ red pepper, de-seeded and chopped
   very finely
2 cox's apples, peeled, cored and diced
2 tablespoons lemon juice
350g (12oz) closed cup mushrooms, sliced
125g (4½ oz) vegetarian blue cheese, crumbled
1 tablespoon chopped fresh basil
4 sheets of filo pastry
75g (3oz) butter, melted
75g (3oz) fresh wholemeal breadcrumbs

## Chargrilled Red Peppers with Mushrooms

*Preparation and cooking time: 40 minutes · Serves 4*

Cover the bulgar wheat with boiling water and leave for 30 minutes. Pre-heat the grill. Meanwhile, halve the peppers, then place, skin-side up, under the pre-heated grill until the skin blisters and blackens. Place the peppers in a bowl, cover with cling film, and leave for 10 minutes. Then remove the seeds and skins. Keep the peppers warm. Drain the bulgar wheat by pressing down on it through a sieve to squeeze out the excess water. Heat the oil and cook the onion and garlic in a covered pan for a minute. Add the remaining ingredients, and then cook over a medium heat for 4 minutes, stirring occasionally. Season to taste. Stir the wheat into the mushroom mixture and heat through. Serve the peppers with the mushroom mixture on top. Garnish with mushrooms and coriander.

**150** kcals

**5** g fat

ⓋⒼ

4 large red peppers
**For the filling:**
50g (2oz) bulgar wheat
1 tablespoon olive oil
1 red onion, chopped finely
2 garlic cloves, chopped
2.5cm (1-inch) piece of fresh root ginger,
   peeled and chopped finely
2 teaspoons ground turmeric
1 or 2 fresh green chillies, de-seeded and
   sliced finely
1 tablespoon garam masala
225g (8oz) open cup mushrooms,
   chopped finely
salt and freshly ground black pepper
**To garnish:**
sautéed sliced mushrooms
sprigs of fresh coriander

**90** kcals

**2** g fat

4 whole acorn squashes

275g (9½oz) closed cup mushrooms, quartered

2 red chillies, seeds removed and
    chopped finely

2 garlic cloves, crushed finely

2 tablespoons chopped fresh sage

2 teaspoons olive oil

fresh sage, to garnish

## Baked Squash filled with Mushrooms

*Preparation time: 10 minutes . Cooking time: 35–40 minutes · Serves 4*

Preheat the oven to Gas 6/200°C/400°F. Trim the bases of each squash so that they stand firm. Cut a slice off the top, then scoop out the seeds. Mix the mushrooms, chillies, garlic and sage together and then use to fill the squash. Drizzle over a little oil. Place on a lightly oiled baking sheet, cover with foil, and bake in the oven for 35–40 minutes. Garnish with sage.

**420** kcals

**25** g fat

**V**

**For the pancake batter:**

125g (4½oz) plain flour

a pinch of salt

1 medium egg, beaten

300ml (½ pint) semi-skimmed milk

1 tablespoon oil

**For the filling:**

a bunch of watercress, washed, drained and
    chopped finely

350g (12oz) closed cup mushrooms, chopped
    very finely

220g carton of ricotta cheese

grated rind of 1 lemon

40g (1½oz) butter, melted

**For the tomato sauce:**

1 tablespoon oil

1 onion, chopped very finely

125g (4½oz) closed cup mushrooms, chopped
    very finely

190ml (7fl oz) water

225g (8oz) vine-ripened tomatoes, peeled
    and chopped finely

3 fresh bay leaves

2 tablespoons tomato purée

2 teaspoons cornflour

a sprig of watercress, to garnish

## Mushroom and Ricotta Parcels

*Preparation time: 40 minutes · Cooking time: 25 minutes · Serves 4*

To make the pancake batter, sift the flour into a bowl. Add the salt, beaten egg and half the milk. Stir in the flour gradually, keeping the mixture free of lumps. Then whisk in the remaining milk. Heat a very small quantity of oil in an omelette pan and use a little of the batter to make a thin pancake. Repeat to make 12 pancakes. Preheat the oven to Gas 4/180°C/350°F. Mix together the filling ingredients, reserving a little melted butter, and divide the mixture between the pancakes. Roll up the pancakes to make neat parcels. Place the parcels, seam-side underneath, in a greased ovenproof dish and brush with the remaining butter. Cover with the foil and cook in the oven for 25 minutes.

Meanwhile, make the tomato sauce. Heat the oil in a pan and cook the onion and mushrooms for three minutes. Stir in the water, tomatoes, bay leaves and tomato purée. Bring to the boil and simmer for 10 minutes. Blend the cornflour with 2 teaspoons of cold water, then stir into the sauce. Bring to the boil, stirring. Discard the bay leaves. Serve the parcels with the tomato sauce. Garnish with a sprig of watercress.

*Mushroom and Ricotta Parcels*

## Mushroom and Aubergine Wheels

*Preparation time: 40 minutes · Cooking time: 20 minutes · Serves 4*

Preheat the oven to Gas 5/190°C/375°F. Heat the oil and cook the mushrooms and leek for 3 minutes. Turn the mushrooms and leek into a bowl with breadcrumbs and orange rind and seasoning. Mix well, then leave to cool. Slice the aubergines lengthways into 12 thin slices. Discard the two end slices. Brush one side of each slice with a little oil, and then place oil-side down on a chopping board. Divide the mushroom mixture between the aubergine slices. Roll up each slice to enclose the filling.

Thread 3 rolls on to each of 8 skewers. Place on a lightly oiled baking tray and cook in the oven, for about 20 minutes. Meanwhile, make the tomato sauce. Heat the oil in a pan, then add the shallots, garlic and tomatoes. Cover and cook over a medium heat for 5 minutes. Add the orange juice, tomato purée and cayenne pepper and cook for a further 5 minutes. Add the basil and stir until the basil wilts. Turn into a food processor and blend until fairly smooth. Return to the pan and keep warm. Serve the aubergine wheels with the sauce.

**155** kcals

**5** g fat

(VG)

1 tablespoon oil
450g (1lb) closed cup mushrooms
1 leek, chopped very finely
50g (2oz) fresh breadcrumbs
grated rind of one orange
2 large aubergines
salt and freshly ground black pepper

**For the tomato sauce:**
1 tablespoon olive oil
2 shallots, chopped
2 garlic cloves, chopped
450g (1lb) vine-ripened tomatoes, peeled and
    chopped
juice of 1 orange
2 tablespoons tomato purée
a pinch of cayenne pepper
15g pack of fresh basil, stems removed from
    the leaves

## Roasted Vegetable Pizza

*Preparation time: 25 minutes · Cooking time: 45 minutes · Serves 4*

Preheat the oven to Gas 5/190°C/375°F. Put the courgette, red pepper, onion and garlic in a roasting tin. Pour over the oil and turn the vegetables until they are well coated. Roast in the oven, for 10 minutes. Stir in mushrooms and roast for a further 15 minutes, stirring occasionally. Remove from the oven, then add the tomatoes and set aside. Turn the oven up to Gas 6/200°C/400°F. Make up the pizza dough according to the pack instructions and roll out to line a 35cm (14-inch) round deep pizza tin or two 28cm (11-inch) round pizza trays. Turn the vegetables on to the dough. Sprinkle with herbs and top with the cheeses. Bake in the oven for about 20 minutes.

**645** kcals

**30** g fat

(V)

175g (6oz) courgette, cut into large sticks
1 large red pepper, de-seeded and cubed
1 red onion, cut into wedge-shaped slices
3 garlic cloves, chopped
3 tablespoons olive oil
225g (8oz) closed cup mushrooms
225g (8oz) open cup mushrooms
350g (12oz) plum tomatoes, chopped roughly
290g packet of pizza base mix
2 tablespoons chopped fresh rosemary
1 tablespoon chopped fresh parsley
125g (4½oz) smoked mozzarella cheese,
    grated
125g (4½oz) Parmesan cheese, grated

**480** kcals

**20** g fat

4 rashers unsmoked back bacon
4 chicken joints, skinned
3 tablespoons flour, seasoned with a pinch
    of salt and pepper
1 teaspoon ground nutmeg
2 tablespoons oil
3 large garlic cloves, chopped finely
300ml (½ pint) red wine
150ml (¼ pint) chicken stock
4 tablespoons chopped fresh parsley
200g pack of horse mushrooms
350g (12oz) brown/chestnut mushrooms, halved

## Chicken and Mushroom Casserole

*Preparation time: 10 minutes · Cooking time: 50 minutes · Serves 4*

Preheat the oven to Gas 4/180°C/350°F. Wrap the bacon around the chicken. Mix together the seasoned flour and nutmeg and then use this to coat the chicken. Heat the oil in a large pan and cook the garlic for 30 seconds. Add the chicken and any remaining flour and cook for a minute, turning the chicken over once. Stir in the wine and stock and bring to the boil stirring. Add the parsley, then transfer to an ovenproof casserole. Cook in the oven for 35 minutes. Stir in the mushrooms and return to the oven for a further 15 minutes.

**180** kcals

**5** g fat

350g (12oz) mixed white or brown mushrooms
125g pack of mixed exotic mushrooms
2 tablespoons groundnut oil
2 garlic cloves, chopped
275g (9½ oz) chicken breast, cut into strips
1 red pepper, de-seeded and sliced
1 bunch of spring onions, sliced
2.5cm (1-inch) piece of fresh root ginger,
    peeled and grated
2 tablespoons soy sauce
2 teaspoons clear honey
1 tablespoon tomato sauce

## Chicken and Mushroom Stir-fry

*Preparation and cooking time: 30 minutes · Serves 4*

Slice the larger mushrooms. Heat the oil in a wok and stir-fry the garlic for 30 seconds. Add the chicken and stir-fry for 5 minutes. Add the pepper, onions, ginger and sliced mushrooms and stir-fry for 8 minutes. Stir in the whole mushrooms, soy sauce, honey and tomato sauce and stir-fry for further 2 minutes. If you like, serve with cooked noodles.

*Chicken and Mushroom Stir-fry*

## Marinated Chicken with Mushrooms

*Preparation time: 5 minutes + 2 hours marinating*
*Cooking time: 15 minutes · Serves 4*

Put the marinade ingredients into a large shallow dish. Make criss-cross cuts over the top of the chicken breasts and then place in the marinade. Cover and leave for 2 hours, turning occasionally. Remove the chicken from the marinade, and then cook under a pre-heated grill for 15 minutes, turning occasionally. Meanwhile, pour the reserved marinade into a saucepan with the broccoli and stock. Cover and cook over a gentle heat for about 3 minutes. Stir in mushrooms and cook for a further 3 minutes until juices begin to run. Stir in crème fraîche and heat through. Serve with the chicken.

4 chicken breast fillets, skinned
300g (10½ oz) trimmed broccoli florets
2 tablespoons stock
250g (9oz) closed cup mushrooms, quartered
200ml carton of half-fat crème fraîche

**For the marinade:**
150ml (¼ pint) white wine
2 garlic cloves, chopped very finely
2 tablespoons chopped fresh rosemary
1½ teaspoons cumin seeds, crushed lightly
freshly ground black pepper

**250** kcals

**10** g fat

## Mushroom and Chestnut Stuffing for Roast Chicken

*Preparation and Cooking time: 10 minutes*

Heat the oil in a pan and cook the onion and mushrooms for 2 minutes. Cool, then transfer to a mixing bowl. Add the remaining ingredients and mix together well. Use to loosely stuff the neck end of the chicken and roast according to the pack instructions. (If stuffing a turkey, you will need to double the quantity.) Shape the remainder of the stuffing into balls. Halfway through cooking the chicken, arrange the stuffing balls around the chicken. If desired, place the extra mushrooms around the roast chicken for the last 10 minutes.

2 teaspoons oil
1 small onion, chopped finely
175g (6oz) brown/chestnut mushrooms, chopped finely
125g (4½ oz) fresh pork mince
25g (1oz) fresh breadcrumbs
75g (3oz) whole peeled chestnuts, chopped finely
2 tablespoons shredded fresh sage
1 small egg, beaten
a handful of brown/chestnut mushrooms (optional)
1.8kg (4lb) chicken

**590** kcals

**30** g fat

Tip: Put some mushrooms around a roast during the last ten minutes of cooking. The mushrooms will absorb the juices and make marvellous gravy. Mushrooms also only need to be added to casseroles towards the end of the cooking time.

main meals

*Marinated Chicken with Mushrooms*

**345** kcals

**20** g fat

4 duck (or game or guinea fowl) breasts, unskinned
1 tablespoon oil
2 garlic cloves, chopped
125g (4½ oz) shallots, quartered
3 × 120g packs of shiitake mushrooms, stalks trimmed
3 tablespoons redcurrant jelly
3 tablespoons Madeira
200ml (7fl oz) hot duck or chicken stock
2 tablespoons shredded fresh mint
2 tablespoons chopped fresh parsley
1 or 2 teaspoons cornflour, blended with a little cold water
salt and freshly ground black pepper

## Duck with Shiitake and Madeira Sauce

*Preparation: 10 minutes · Cooking: 25 minutes · Serves 4*

Preheat the oven to Gas 6/200°C/400°F. Prick the duck skin all over with a fork. Heat the oil in a frying pan and cook the garlic and shallots until just beginning to brown. Transfer to a roasting tin. Put the duck breasts, skin-side down, into the frying pan and cook until the fat just begins to run. Increase the heat to brown the skin, then transfer the duck breasts to a rack over the shallots in the roasting tin. Roast in the oven for 10 minutes. Remove from the oven and stir the shiitake mushrooms into the shallots. Return to the oven and roast for a further 10 minutes. Transfer the duck to a warm plate and leave to rest while making the sauce.

Drain off the excess fat from the roasting tin, and then transfer the roasting tin to the hob. Stir in the redcurrant jelly, Madeira, stock and herbs and cook over a medium heat for about 3 minutes. Stir in the blended cornflour and bring to the boil until sauce is just thickened. Season to taste. Slice each duck breast and fan out on to warm serving plates. Spoon over the mushroom sauce and garnish with fresh mint.

**285** kcals

**10** g fat

2 tablespoons oil
12 baby onions
350g (12oz) lean braising steak, cubed
3 tablespoons flour seasoned with a pinch of salt and pepper
250ml (9 fl oz) beef stock
2 tablespoons Worcestershire sauce
1 tablespoon horseradish mustard
2 large carrots, sliced thickly
575g (1¼lb) open cup mushrooms, halved

## Devilled Mushroom and Beef Casserole

*Preparation time: 20 minutes · Cooking time: 1½ hours · Serves 4*

Heat the oil in a large saucepan and brown the onions. Coat the beef in the seasoned flour and then add it to the pan. Cook for a minute, stirring. Gradually stir in the stock, Worcestershire sauce and mustard. Bring to the boil, stirring. Add the carrots, cover and simmer for 1¼ hours. Stir in the mushrooms, cover and simmer for a further 15 minutes.

*Duck with Shiitake and Madeira Sauce*

## Japanese Pork Teriyaki with Mushrooms

*Preparation and cooking time: 3 hours marinating + 5 minutes · Serves 4*

Mix the teriyaki, red wine and stock together in a large bowl. Add the mushrooms and pork to the marinade and mix well. Cover and leave for 3 hours, stirring occasionally. Transfer to a large saucepan with the juices. Cover and cook over a high heat for about 5 minutes, stirring occasionally. Stir in the spring onions and cook for a minute. Lift out the pork and vegetables and keep warm. Reduce the liquor to about 6 tablespoons by rapid boiling. Meanwhile cook the noodles according to the pack instructions. Put the noodles in bowls, top with the pork and mushrooms. Pour the liquor over and scatter on the sesame seeds.

3 tablespoons teriyaki sauce
4 tablespoons red wine
2 tablespoons stock
100g pack of enoki mushrooms
200g pack of horse mushrooms, sliced
2 × 120g packs of shiitake mushrooms
450g (1lb) lean pork fillet, cut into thin slices
a bunch of spring onions, shredded finely
1 tablespoon sesame seeds, toasted
250g packet of egg noodles

**455** kcals
**10** g fat

## Chinese Sweet 'n Sour Pork

*Preparation time: 10 minutes · Cooking time: 1hr 35 minutes · Serves 4*

Preheat the oven to Gas 3/170°C/325°F. Mix together the seasoned flour and five-spice seasoning in a bowl. Toss the pork in the seasoned flour to coat thoroughly. Heat the oil in a wok and cook the garlic and ginger for 30 seconds. Stir in the pork and cook until browned. Gradually stir in the pineapple juice and slowly bring to the boil, stirring. Transfer to a casserole dish, cover and cook in the oven for 1¼ hours. Stir in the remaining ingredients and return to the oven for 15 minutes.

2 tablespoons flour seasoned with a pinch of
   salt and pepper
2 teaspoons Chinese five-spice seasoning
450g (1lb) lean pork, cubed
2 tablespoons oil
2 garlic cloves, chopped finely
2cm (¾-inch) piece of fresh root ginger, peeled
   and chopped finely
300ml (½ pint) pineapple juice
450g (1lb) closed cup mushrooms, halved
125g pack of oyster mushrooms, torn
75g (3oz) small mange-tout peas
2 tablespoons soy sauce
2 tablespoons white wine vinegar
a bunch of spring onions, sliced thickly

**290** kcals
**10** g fat

*Japanese Pork Teriyaki with Mushrooms (top), Chinese Sweet 'n Sour Pork*

**410** kcals

**25** g fat

4 lamb steaks
2 tablespoons olive oil
450g (1lb) closed cup mushrooms, quartered
250g (9oz) couscous

**For the marinade:**
1 teaspoon cumin seeds, crushed lightly
grated rind and juice of 1 lemon
3 garlic cloves, chopped finely
1 tablespoon set honey
1 tablespoon harissa paste

**To garnish:**
lemon wedges
chopped fresh coriander

## Moroccan Lamb Steaks with Mushrooms

*Preparation time: 10 minutes + 4 hours marinating*
*Cooking time: 15 minutes · Serves 4*

Mix the marinade ingredients together in a bowl. Make two or three slashes in each lamb steak. Press some of the marinade into each cut, then place the steaks in a shallow dish, with the remaining marinade poured over. Cover and leave to marinate for at least 4 hours. Lift the steaks out of the marinade, and then grill for 12 to 15 minutes, turning over once, half-way through the cooking. Meanwhile, heat the oil in a frying pan and quickly fry the mushrooms for 2 minutes, stirring. Cook the couscous according to the pack instructions. Add the remaining marinade to the mushrooms, reduce the heat, and cook for 5 minutes. Serve the lamb with the mushrooms and couscous. Garnish with lemon wedges and coriander.

**275** kcals

**15** g fat

350g (12oz) neck fillet of lamb, cut into
    small cubes
1 tablespoon oil
1 green pepper, de-seeded and cut into strips
1 red chilli pepper, de-seeded and sliced thinly
675g (1½ lb) closed cup mushrooms, sliced
2 tablespoons tomato purée

**For the marinade:**
6 tablespoons natural yoghurt
1 teaspoon ground cumin
2 teaspoons ground coriander
½–1 teaspoon chilli powder
1 teaspoon garam masala
2 garlic cloves, chopped finely
1 tablespoon lemon juice

## Balti Lamb with Mushrooms

*Preparation time: 15 minutes + 4 hours marinating*
*Cooking time: 15 minutes · Serves 4*

Mix the marinade ingredients together in a bowl. Stir in the lamb. Cover and leave to marinate for at least 4 hours. Heat the oil in a deep, round-bottomed frying pan, (karahi) or wok. Add the lamb, leaving the excess marinade in the bowl. Cook the lamb for 7 minutes, stirring frequently. Stir in the peppers, cook for a minute and then stir in the mushrooms and tomato purée. Cook for a further 4 minutes, stirring frequently.

*Moroccan Lamb Steaks with Mushrooms*

## Roasted Sea Bass with Oyster Mushroom Sauce

*Preparation time: 15 minutes · Cooking time: 20 minutes · Serves 4*

Preheat the oven to Gas 4/180°C/350°F. Make five slits on each side of each fish, and then place some garlic in each slit. Put the lime slices into the body cavity of each fish. Arrange the fish in a roasting tin and drizzle over a little olive oil. Roast in the oven, for about 20 minutes, or until the fish is cooked. Meanwhile, to make the sauce, heat the oil in a pan and quickly brown the shallots and mushrooms. Stir in the flour and cook for a minute. Gradually stir in the wine and tarragon. Bring to the boil, then stir in the cream and heat thoroughly, stirring, but do not allow to boil. Serve the sea bass with the oyster mushroom sauce and garnish with lime and tarragon.

4 × 350g (12oz) sea bass, cleaned
3–4 garlic cloves, chopped finely
2 limes, sliced
olive oil, for drizzling
**For the sauce:**
2 tablespoons oil
2 shallots, chopped finely
2 × 125g packs of oyster mushrooms,
    larger ones torn
1 tablespoon flour
200ml (7fl oz) dry white wine
2 tablespoons roughly chopped fresh tarragon
142ml carton of double cream
**To garnish:**
lime wedges
fresh tarragon

630 kcals
35 g fat

## Salmon with Mushroom Salsa

*Preparation time: 15 minutes · Cooking time: 15 minutes · Serves 4*

Preheat the grill. Brush the salmon steaks with honey, then grill for 12 to 15 minutes, turning the steaks over once, halfway through the cooking. Meanwhile mix all the ingredients together for the salsa in a bowl or put them in a food processor and blend until finely chopped. Serve the salmon with the mushroom salsa and lightly sautéed mushrooms.

4 salmon steaks
4 teaspoons clear honey
**For the salsa:**
200g pack of button mushrooms, chopped
    very finely
2–3 green chilli peppers, de-seeded and
    chopped very finely
1 red pepper, de-seeded and chopped
    very finely
4 large spring onions, chopped very finely
grated rind and juice of 1 lime
675g (1½ lb) closed cup mushrooms, fluted
25g (1oz) butter
1 tablespoon sunflower oil

315 kcals
15 g fat

Tip: To 'flute' mushrooms for special occasions, make a series of curved cuts from the top of each mushroom cap to the base. Remove a narrow strip of skin along each cut.

*Salmon with Mushroom Salsa*

380 kcals

15 g fat

2 tablespoons oil
2 garlic cloves, chopped very finely
3 chicken breast fillets, skinned and cubed
200g pack of button mushrooms, halved
½ red pepper, de-seeded and diced
50g (2oz) baby corn, sliced thickly
2 tablespoons chopped fresh parsley
150ml (¼ pint) dry white wine
2 tablespoons cornflour
12 taco shells
lime wedges

## Mexican Chicken and Mushroom Tacos

*Preparation and Cooking time: 20 minutes · Serves 4*

Heat the oil and cook the garlic and chicken for 3 minutes. Stir in the mushrooms and red pepper and cook for a further 2 minutes. Add the baby corn, parsley and wine. Bring to the boil, stirring. Blend the cornflour with a little cold water, then stir it into the pan to thicken the juices. Cook for another minute. Meanwhile, heat the taco shells according to the pack instructions, then spoon the chicken mixture into tacos. Serve with lime wedges.

suppers

*Mexican Chicken and Mushroom Tacos*

## Grilled Polenta with Mushrooms and Smoked Haddock

*Preparation and Cooking time: 15 minutes · Serves 4*

Heat the oil in a large saucepan. Add the mushrooms and cook for a minute, stirring. Turn down the heat and add the crème fraîche, mustard, parsley and smoked haddock. Stir well, cover and cook over a gentle heat for about 6 minutes. Cook the polenta under a pre-heated grill for about 3 minutes on each side. Serve the polenta with the mushrooms and smoked haddock.

2 tablespoons olive oil
450g (1lb) open cup mushrooms
4 tablespoons crème fraîche
1½ teaspoons Dijon mustard
4 tablespoons chopped fresh parsley
225g (8oz) smoked haddock, skinned and cubed
250g packet of ready-to-use polenta, cut into 8 thick fingers

**455** kcals
**20** g fat

## Mushroomy Spaghetti Bolognese

*Preparation time: 10 minutes · Cooking time: 15 minutes · Serves 4*

Cook the beef, onion and garlic in a covered saucepan over a medium heat for 5 minutes, stirring occasionally. Stir in the mushrooms, tomatoes, herbs and tomato purée. Bring to the boil, and then simmer gently for 10 minutes, stirring occasionally. Meanwhile cook the spaghetti according to the pack instructions. Drain the spaghetti and divide between four plates. Spoon over the sauce and sprinkle on the grated cheese.

225g (8oz) fresh minced beef
1 large onion, chopped
2 garlic cloves, chopped finely
575g (1¼ lb) closed cup mushrooms, chopped roughly
400g can peeled chopped tomatoes
4 teaspoons chopped fresh mixed herbs
3 tablespoons tomato purée
450g (1lb) spaghetti
grated Parmesan cheese, to serve

**550** kcals
**10** g fat

Tip: Make your meals go further:
add sliced fresh mushrooms to chilled pasta sauces to create more servings or reduce the quantity of meat in a dish and add some roughly chopped mushrooms.

suppers

51

*Grilled Polenta with Mushrooms and Smoked Haddock*

**385** kcals
**20** g fat

2 tablespoons sesame oil
25g (1oz) butter
2 garlic cloves, chopped finely
1 tablespoon sesame seeds
2 tablespoons chopped fresh rosemary
125g pack of blewit mushrooms
150g pack of button mushrooms
125g (4½oz) closed cup mushrooms
200g pack of horse mushrooms
125g pack of oyster mushrooms
2 tablespoons white wine or light stock
250g (9oz) medium egg noodles
salt and freshly ground black pepper

## Mixed Mushrooms with Noodles

*Preparation and Cooking time: 20 minutes · Serves 4*

Heat the oil and butter together in a large saucepan. Add the garlic, sesame seeds and rosemary and cook for 30 seconds. Halve any large mushrooms then add all the mushrooms to the pan. Cover and cook for 3 minutes, stirring occasionally. Add the wine and cook over a gentle heat for a further minute. Season to taste. Meanwhile cook the egg noodles according to the pack instructions and drain. Stir the egg noodles into the mushrooms. Serve immediately.

**505** kcals
**12** g fat

500g pack of fresh pasta shells
225g (8oz) asparagus, cut into 7.5cm (3-inch)
    lengths
1 tablespoon olive oil
2 garlic cloves, chopped very finely
350g (12oz) closed cup mushrooms, sliced
4 tablespoons vegetable stock
2 tablespoons chopped fresh thyme
150g (5½oz) half-fat Cheddar cheese, grated
freshly ground black pepper

## Pasta with Mushrooms and Asparagus

*Preparation and cooking time: 15 minutes · Serves 4*

Cook the pasta according to the pack instructions. Meanwhile, cook the asparagus stems in boiling water for 2 minutes. Add the asparagus tips and cook for a further minute. Drain. Heat the oil and cook the garlic and mushrooms for a minute, stirring. Add the vegetable stock, black pepper and thyme. Cover and cook for 2 minutes. Add the asparagus and heat gently. Fold in the cooked, drained pasta and most of the cheese. Serve immediately with the remaining cheese sprinkled on top.

Tip: The 'holy trinity' of fat-free mushroom cooking is 240 ml stock, 120 ml wine and a dash of teriyaki sauce. Use this to poach or microwave your mushrooms and see how well it brings out their flavour.

*Mixed Mushrooms with Noodles (top), Pasta with Mushrooms and Asparagus*

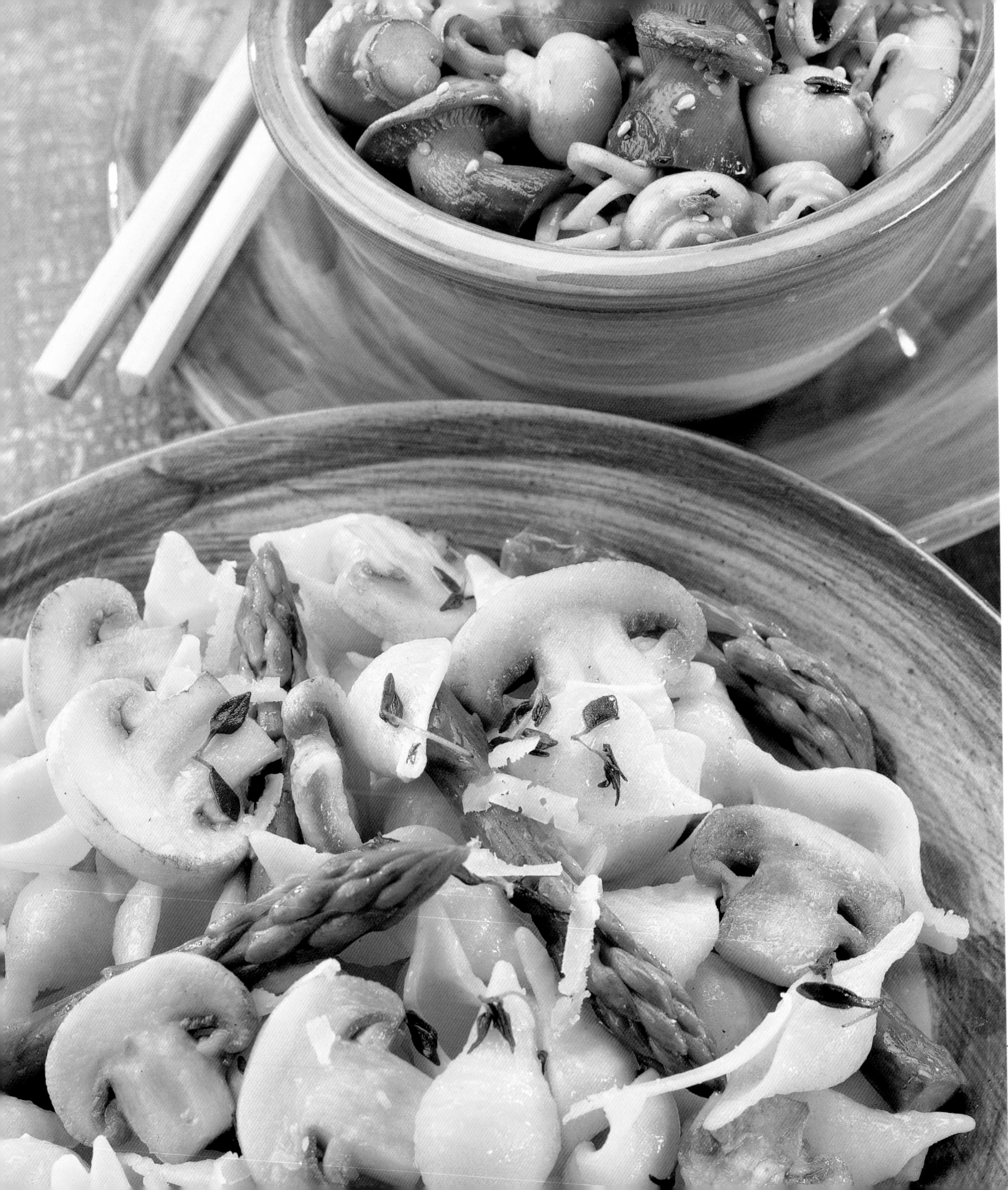

## Pasta with Mushrooms and Pesto Sauce

*Preparation and Cooking time: 15 minutes · Serves 2*

Cook the pasta according to the pack instructions. Spoon the crème fraîche into a large pan with the pesto. Heat gently. Add the sliced mushrooms. Bring slowly to the boil and simmer for 5 minutes. Stir the mushroom sauce into the cooked and drained pasta.

250g pack of fresh pasta
250ml carton of crème fraîche
4 teaspoons ready-made pesto
350g (12oz) closed cup mushrooms,
    sliced thickly

**790** kcals

**45** g fat

(V)

## Skewered Mushrooms with Bacon and Turkey

*Preparation time: 25 minutes · Cooking time: 15 minutes · Makes 8*

Preheat the oven to Gas 4/180°C/350°F. Heat the oil and cook the shallots until soft. Turn into a bowl with the turkey, herbs, breadcrumbs, beaten egg and seasoning and mix well. Use the mixture to sandwich the mushrooms together in pairs. Wrap each one in a bacon rasher and secure with small skewers. Cook in the oven for about 15 minutes, turning and brushing with oil regularly.

1 tablespoon oil
2 shallots, chopped finely
175g (6oz) fresh turkey mince
1 tablespoon chopped fresh parsley
1 tablespoon chopped thyme
1 tablespoon chopped sage
50g (2oz) fresh breadcrumbs
1 small egg, beaten
16 large even-sized open cup mushrooms,
    stalks cut level
8 rashers of rindless streaky bacon, stretched
    with the back of a knife
oil, for brushing
salt and freshly ground black pepper

**130** kcals

**10** g fat

*Skewered Mushrooms with Bacon and Turkey*

**265** kcals

**10** g fat

4 large flat or portabello mushrooms
4 teaspoons sunflower oil
4 wafer-thin Cheddar slices
4 baps
110g bag of washed and ready-to-eat mixed
  salad leaves
300g jar of sweetcorn, tomato or onion relish
slices of lean bacon (optional)

## Quick Grilled Mushroom Burger

*Preparation and Cooking time: 10 minutes · Serves 4*

If using, fry the bacon. Brush each mushroom lightly with oil and grill for 3 minutes. Turn over and grill for a further 2 minutes. Meanwhile, put a cheese slice on one half of each bap and grill until the cheese begins to melt. Top each bap half with a mushroom, some salad leaves, a spoonful of relish, the bacon, if using, and the other half of the bap.

**430** kcals

**20** g fat

Ⓥ

250g (9oz) couscous
2 large carrots, sliced
1 tablespoon olive oil
1 red onion, cut into wedges
2 garlic cloves, chopped finely
275g (9½oz) open cup mushrooms
227g can of bamboo shoots
220g can of water chestnuts
125g (4½oz) cashew nuts, toasted
2 teaspoons Chinese five-spice seasoning
2 tablespoons sherry
2 tablespoons soy sauce
3 tablespoons chopped fresh coriander

## Eastern Mushroom and Vegetable Couscous

*Preparation and cooking time: 30 minutes · Serves 4*

Cook the couscous according to the packet instructions. Cook the carrots in boiling water for 2 minutes, and then drain. Heat the oil in a large saucepan and cook the onion and garlic for a minute. Add the mushrooms, cover and continue to cook for 2 minutes. Stir in the remaining ingredients and continue cooking for about 4 minutes. Stir in the cooked couscous for the last minute.

Tip: Add sliced mushrooms to stir-fries for the last couple of minutes – one always seems to end up with less than expected and mushrooms can bump up the volume!

*Eastern Mushroom and Vegetable Couscous*

## Mushrooms Topped with Goats' Cheese and Ham

*Preparation and Cooking time: 30 minutes · Makes 4*

Preheat the oven to Gas 5/190°C/375°F. Melt the butter and oil together in a large frying pan. Add the paprika pepper and cook for a few seconds. Add the mushrooms and cook on both sides for about a minute. Oil four large squares of foil. Place each mushroom, gill-side up, on a piece of foil. Place a slice of ham, some goats' cheese and parsley on each mushroom. Drizzle the remaining oil and paprika over the top. Fold the foil to make loose parcels, sealing the edges together well. Cook in the oven for 12 minutes. Remove from foil and serve immediately.

40g (1½ oz) unsalted butter

3 tablespoons olive oil

4 teaspoons paprika pepper

4 large flat or portabello mushrooms

4 slices honey roast ham, folded in half

100g packet of goats' cheese cut into four
    round slices

3 tablespoons chopped fresh flat-leaf parsley

2 teaspoons oil, for greasing

**235** kcals

**20** g fat

## Spicy Potato Wedges with Mushrooms

*Preparation time: 10 minutes · Cooking time: 50 minutes · Serves 2*

Cook the potatoes in boiling water for a minute, then drain well. Heat the oil in a roasting tin and fry the spices for 30 seconds. Add the potatoes and stir well to coat. Cook in the oven at Gas Mark 6/200°C/400°F for 25 minutes, stirring once half-way through the cooking. Stir in the mushrooms, corn and leeks and cook for a further 20 minutes. Stir, sprinkle the cheese over the top and cook for a further 5 minutes.

450g (1lb) potatoes, scrubbed then cut into
    fairly thick wedges

2 tablespoons olive oil

2 teaspoons paprika pepper

2 teaspoons ground cumin

1 teaspoon ground coriander

1 teaspoon ground tumeric

250g (9oz) brown/chestnut mushrooms, halved

125g (4½ oz) baby corn

2 small leeks, sliced thickly

75g (3oz) Red Leicester cheese, grated

**475** kcals

**25** g fat

*Mushrooms Topped with Goats' Cheese and Ham*

290 kcals

9 g fat

175g (6oz) long grain rice
a bunch of chives, snipped
200g pack of button mushrooms, sliced thinly
1 large carrot, grated
1 small fennel bulb, sliced thinly
35g pack of rocket leaves
3 tablespoons tapenade
200ml carton of half-fat crème fraîche

## Mushroom and Rice Salad with Tapenade Sauce

*Preparation time: 15 minutes · Cooking time: 15 minutes · Serves 4*

Cook the rice according to the packet instructions. Rinse the cooked rice under cold running water and drain well. Turn the rice into a bowl and add the chives, mushrooms, carrot and fennel. Toss in the rice and mix everything together. Spoon on to plates lined with rocket leaves. Stir the tapenade into the crème fraîche and then spoon the sauce over the rice salad.

80 kcals

1 g fat

2 × 150g packs of button mushrooms
100g pack of enoki mushrooms
juice of 1 large lime
3 tablespoons chopped fresh mint
425g (15oz) ripe and ready-to-eat pineapple
1 large ripe pawpaw, peeled, halved and seeds removed
crisp lettuce leaves

**To garnish:**
wedges of lime
sprigs of fresh mint

## Mushroom, Pineapple and Pawpaw Salad

*Preparation time: 5 minutes · Serves 4*

Put the mushrooms in a large bowl with the lime juice and mint. Stir well. Slice the pineapple into thick rounds, remove the core, cut into wedges, and then add to the mushrooms. Slice the pawpaw and gently fold into the salad. Serve on lettuce, garnished with lime wedges and mint.

salads

*Mushroom, Pineapple and Pawpaw Salad*

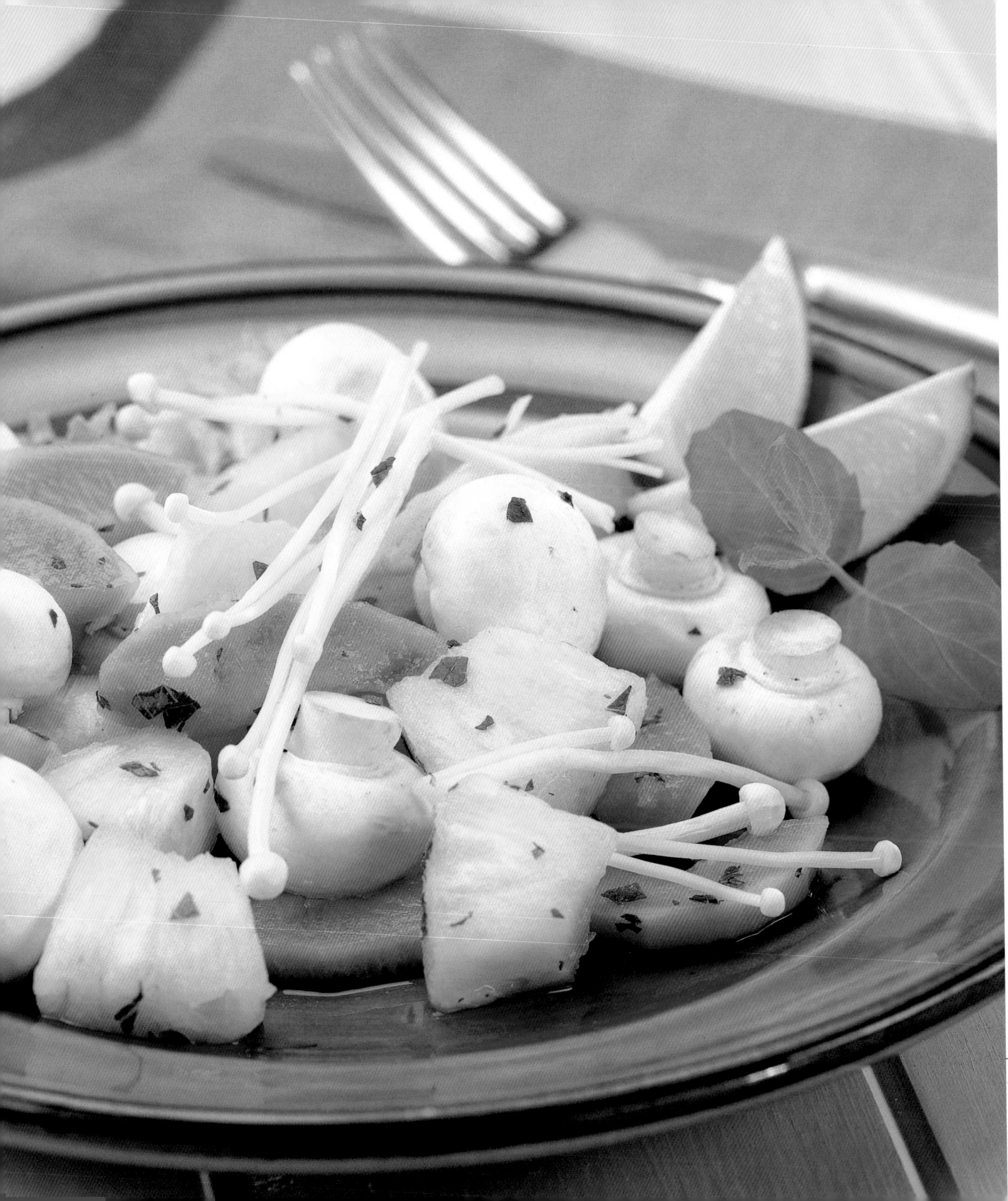

## Warm Smoked Chicken, Mushroom and Hazelnut Salad

*Preparation time: 15 minutes · Cooking time: 25 minutes · Serves 4*

Toast the hazelnuts and cool. Mix the toasted hazelnuts with the remaining dressing ingredients. Cook the potatoes in boiling salted water for about 10 minutes, or until tender. Cook the fresh peas in boiling salted water for 4 minutes or the frozen peas for 3 minutes. Meanwhile, heat the oil in a large pan and stir-fry the mushrooms and chicken for 3 minutes. Drain the potatoes and peas and transfer to a large salad bowl with the lettuce and spring onions. Add the mushrooms and chicken. Pour over the dressing and toss together before serving.

675g (1½ lb) baby new potatoes
450g (1lb) fresh peas, shelled or 225g (8oz) frozen
2 tablespoons sunflower oil
350g (12oz) closed cup mushrooms, sliced thickly
450g (1lb) ready-cooked smoked or chargrilled chicken pieces
1 little gem lettuce, torn into pieces
3 spring onions, cut into fine shreds

**For the dressing:**
50g (2oz) chopped hazelnuts
5 tablespoons olive oil
1½ tablespoons white wine vinegar
1 garlic clove, crushed
¼ teaspoon fresh coarsely ground black pepper

**655** kcals
**35** g fat

## Mushroom and Watercress Salad Tossed in Chilli Dressing

*Preparation time: 15 minutes · Serves 4*

Whisk all the ingredients for the dressing together in a small bowl. Toss the mushrooms, tomato, watercress and lettuce into a salad bowl and then pour over the dressing. Mix gently to coat well. Arrange the salami on plates with the salad.

2 × 150g packs of button mushrooms
one large beef tomato, peeled and cubed
75g (3oz) watercress, washed
½ crisp lettuce, washed and torn into small pieces
70g pack of Milano sliced salami

**For the dressing:**
4 tablespoons extra-virgin olive oil
3 tablespoons white wine vinegar
1–2 dried chilli peppers, crushed
freshly ground black pepper

**200** kcals
**20** g fat

**Tip:** You don't need to peel mushrooms or remove their stalks.
If stuffing the larger mushrooms, it's a good idea to trim the stalks off near the gills.
To slice mushrooms, slice downward from the cap to the stalk.

*Warm Smoked Chicken, Mushroom and Hazelnut Salad*

**160** kcals

**12** g fat

225g (8oz) ready prepared cabbage and carrot
   coleslaw mix
½ Galia melon, seeds removed and either
   cut into cubes or shaped into balls
4 spring onions, sliced thinly
350g (12oz) brown/chestnut mushrooms,
   sliced thinly
**For the dressing:**
2 tablespoons chopped stem ginger
   +1 tablespoon syrup from jar
4 tablespoons grapeseed oil
1 tablespoons white wine vinegar

## Melon and Mushroom Salad in Ginger Dressing

*Preparation time: 15 minutes · Serves 4*

Mix the ingredients for the dressing together. Put the remaining salad ingredients into a large bowl and pour over the dressing. Carefully toss together until all the ingredients are well coated.

**310** kcals

**24** g fat

oil, for deep-frying
3 thick slices of white bread, crusts removed
   and cubed
100g (3½ oz) asparagus tips
6 tablespoons olive oil
2 tablespoons red wine vinegar
1 tablespoon balsamic vinegar
1 teaspoon mustard seed
350g (12oz) closed cup mushrooms, quartered
1 red onion, sliced
110g packet of washed and ready-to-eat
   continental-style salad leaves

## Mushroom and Asparagus Salad

*Preparation time: 5 minutes · Cooking time: 5 minutes · Serves 4*

Heat the oil and cook the bread until golden brown to make croûtons. Drain the croûtons on kitchen paper. Poach the asparagus until just tender then cut each spear into three. Whisk the olive oil, vinegars and mustard seed together then pour over the mushrooms. Stir until well coated. Add the red onion and salad leaves and toss everything together. Sprinkle over the croûtons.

Tip: Mushrooms cook well in the microwave. It only takes three or four minutes to cook a pound of mushrooms on full power. Before cooking, add either a little garlic butter or, for slimmers, a tablespoon of vegetable stock to the dish. Then cover with cling film, leaving a small vent at the side of the dish to allow the steam to escape while cooking.

*Melon and Mushroom Salad in Ginger Dressing*

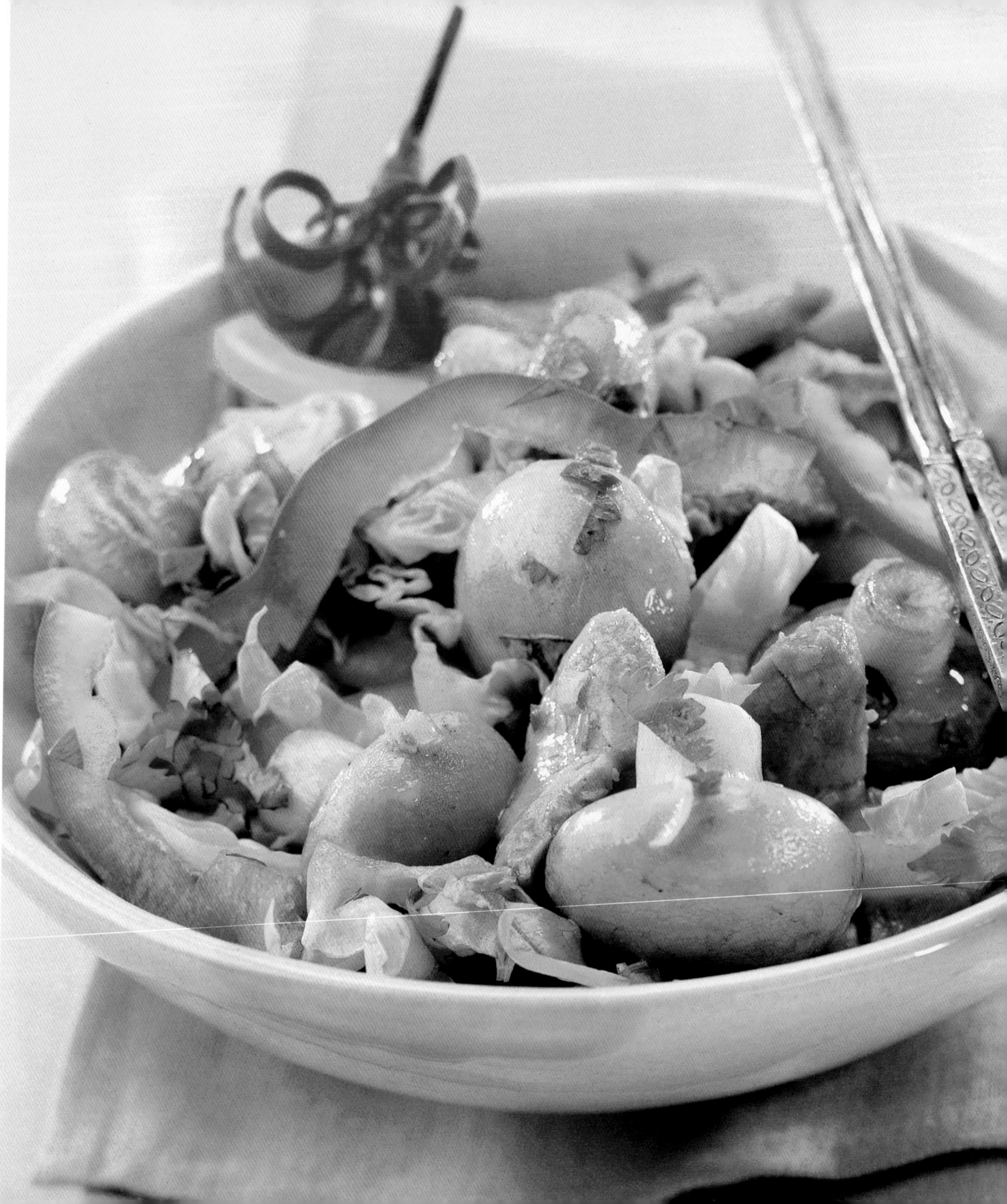

## Thai Mushroom Salad

*Preparation and cooking time: 4 hours marinating + 30 minutes · Serves 4*

Mix the marinade ingredients together. Add the pork to the marinade and mix well. Cover and chill for about 4 hours. Heat the oil in a large frying pan, add the pork and the marinade and cook for about 5 minutes. Stir in the mushrooms and cook for a further minute. Lift out the pork and mushrooms. Reduce the liquor by half by boiling rapidly. Cool. Mix the remaining ingredients together in a large salad bowl. Add the pork and mushrooms. Pour over the cooled liquor and toss together.

450g (1lb) tenderloin pork, sliced thinly
2 tablespoons oil
2 × 200g packs of button mushrooms
1 baby cos lettuce, shredded
3 tablespoons chopped fresh coriander
1 red pepper, de-seeded and cut into
   matchsticks
1 yellow pepper, de-seeded and cut
   into matchsticks

**For the marinade:**
2 tablespoons nam pla
2 tablespoons olive oil
grated rind and juice of 1 lime
1 stick of lemon grass, chopped very finely
1–2 hot red chilli peppers, de-seeded and
   chopped very finely
2 garlic cloves, chopped very finely

**300** kcals

**20** g fat

## Chilled Cheese and Mushroom Salad

*Preparation time: 2 hours freezing + 10 minutes · Serves 4*

Coarsely grate the frozen cheese. Put all the remaining ingredients into a salad bowl and toss together lightly. Drizzle with a little olive oil before serving.

110g pack of smoked brie cheese, frozen
   for 2 hours
½ cucumber, peeled and sliced thinly
1 red onion, sliced thinly
15g pack of fresh basil, torn into small pieces
½ Webb's lettuce, torn into small pieces
2 × 150g packs of baby button mushrooms
coarsely ground black pepper
extra-virgin olive oil

**125** kcals

**10** g fat

(V)

Tip: Mushrooms are satisfying in salads because they have less water in them than other salad vegetables.

*Thai Mushroom Salad*

**700** kcals

**25** g fat

1 tablespoon olive oil

225g (8oz) large fresh prawns, peeled

500g pack of fresh pasta, cooked, drained and
　　rinsed under cold running water

2 × 200g packs of button mushrooms, halved

250g (9oz) cherry tomatoes, halved

15g pack of fresh basil, torn into large pieces

whole prawns, to garnish (optional)

**For the dressing:**

3 tablespoons extra-virgin olive oil

3 tablespoons lemon juice

3 tablespoons pesto

## Mushrooms and Prawns with Pesto and Lemon Dressing

*Preparation and Cooking time: 30 minutes · Serves 4*

Heat the oil and cook the prawns for about 4 minutes, turning them
over after 2 minutes. Allow the prawns to cool. Put the cooked pasta,
mushrooms and tomatoes into a large bowl with the prawns. Whisk all
the dressing ingredients together and then pour over the mushrooms,
tomatoes and prawns. Gently toss until well coated. Scatter the basil
over the top. Garnish with cooked prawns in their shells, if desired.

**580** kcals

**40** g fat

3 tablespoons olive oil

450g (1lb) closed cup mushrooms, quartered

175g (6oz) long grain rice, cooked and drained

225g packet of smoked mackerel fillets,
　　skinned and cubed

1 red pepper, de-seeded and cubed

3 medium eggs, hard-boiled and cut into
　　wedges

1 frisée lettuce, torn into small pieces

**For the dressing:**

2 tablespoons olive oil

2 tablespoons rice vinegar

grated rind and juice of 1 small lemon

## Mushroom and Mackerel Salad in Lemon Dressing

*Preparation and cooking time: 35 minutes · Serves 4*

Whisk the dressing ingredients together. Heat the oil and quickly cook the
mushrooms for 5 minutes. Drain and cool. Carefully mix the remaining
salad ingredients together in a large salad bowl. Add the mushrooms with
the dressing, and toss together lightly.

Tip: Use raw mushrooms with dips instead of crisps –
this makes a much healthier snack!

*Mushrooms and Prawns with Pesto and Lemon Dressing*

## Warm Exotic Mushroom Salad

*Preparation and cooking time: 15 minutes · Serves 4*

Peel and segment one of the oranges. Gently break up the cluster of hon-shimeji mushrooms. Heat the oil in a large frying pan. Add all the mushrooms and cook for 5 minutes. Add the sesame seeds and the grated rind and juice of the remaining orange. Stir in the orange segments and spinach. Heat through, then serve immediately.

2 oranges
150g pack of hon-shimeji mushrooms
3 tablespoons sunflower oil
225g (8oz) brown/chestnut mushrooms, sliced thickly
125g pack of oyster mushrooms
2 tablespoons sesame seeds, toasted
75g (3oz) baby leaf spinach

140 kcals
10 g fat
(VG)

## Lemon and Lime Mushrooms with Smoked Trout

*Preparation time: 15 minutes + 2 hours marinating · Serves 4*

Whisk the ingredients for the dressing together in a large bowl. Add the mushrooms and leave to marinate for about two hours. Add the remaining ingredients, then arrange on individual plates.

450g (1lb) closed cup mushrooms, quartered
½ cucumber, peeled and sliced thinly
150g packet of smoked trout, cut into strips
freshly ground black pepper
**For the dressing:**
juice of 1 small lemon
grated rind and juice of 1 lime
3 tablespoons extra-virgin olive oil
1 teaspoon clear honey
2 tablespoons chopped fresh tarragon

152 kcals
10 g fat

Tip: To make a delicious side dish with mushrooms, pour a little low-calorie French dressing over sliced button mushrooms and chill for three hours. Sprinkle with sesame seeds and chopped fresh herbs and serve.

salads

71

*Warm Exotic Mushroom Salad*

**78** kcals
each

**3** g fat
each

(VG)

8 large flat or portabello mushrooms
oil, for greasing
**For the stuffing:**
3 tablespoons soy sauce
1 tablespoon clear honey
3 tablespoons chopped fresh parsley
400g can of chickpeas, drained
16 pitted green olives, quartered

## Vegetarian Stuffed Mushrooms

*Preparation time: 10 minutes · Cooking time: 10–15 minutes · Makes 8*

If using the oven, preheat it to Gas 5/190°C/375°F. To make the stuffing, mix the soy sauce, honey and parsley together. Stir in the chickpeas and olives. Place the mushrooms on large squares of lightly oiled foil. Spoon the filling mixture on to each mushroom. Fold the foil to make loose parcels, sealing the edges together well. Cook on the barbecue or in the oven for 10–15 minutes.

*Vegetarian Stuffed Mushrooms*

## Barbecued Stuffed Mushrooms with Chorizo and Gruyère

*Preparation time: 20 minutes · Cooking time: 15 minutes · Makes 8*

If using the oven, preheat it to Gas 5/190°C/375°F. Cook the spinach in a covered pan for about 2 minutes. Drain and squeeze out the excess water through a sieve, then roughly chop the spinach. Transfer to a bowl with the tomatoes, chorizo and cheese and mix well. Place the mushrooms on large squares of lightly oiled foil. Spoon the filling mixture on to each mushroom. Fold the foil to make loose parcels, sealing the edges together well. Cook on the barbecue or in the oven for about 15 minutes.

olive oil, for greasing
8 large flat or portabello mushrooms
**For the filling:**
125g (4½oz) baby spinach, washed and
    chopped roughly
75g (3oz) baby plum tomatoes, quartered
70g pack of sliced chorizo, cut into strips
125g (4½oz) Gruyère cheese, cut into
    small cubes

**100** kcals
each

**5** g fat
each

## Barbecued Fish with Mushroom Stuffing

*Preparation time: 15 minutes · Cooking time: 15 minutes · Makes 4*

Preheat the grill if using. Mix the mushrooms, shallots, grated rind and lime juice together. Use half this mixture to stuff the fish and keep the remainder for the side salad. Put the fish in barbecue wire baskets or wrap in lightly oiled foil. Cook on the barbecue or under a moderate grill for 10–15 minutes on each side. Serve with wedges of lime. Add some salad leaves to the remaining mushrooms to make the salad.

175g (6oz) closed cup mushrooms, chopped
175g (6oz) brown/chestnut mushrooms,
    sliced thinly
2 shallots, sliced thinly
grated rind of 1 lime
juice of 2 limes
4 tilapa, red snapper or grey mullet, gutted
    and scored diagonally
mixed salad leaves
wedges of lime, to serve

**235** kcals
each

**4** g fat
each

**Tip:** Always marinate mushrooms well before you barbecue them, especially mushroom kebabs. Try a mixture of two tablespoons of oil and two tablespoons of soy sauce.

barbecues

*Barbecued Fish with Mushroom Stuffing*

**150** kcals each

**10** g fat each

200g packet of blue brie cheese
1 small red pepper, de-seeded and
    chopped finely
24 small open cup mushrooms, stalks cut level
2 tomatoes, each cut into 4 wedges
**For the honey barbecue glaze:**
1 tablespoon clear honey
1 tablespoon oil
1 tablespoon soy sauce

## Mushroom and Cheese Kebabs

*Preparation and Cooking time: 15 minutes · Makes 4 kebabs*

If using the oven, preheat to Gas 5/190°C/375°F. Mix the cheese and red pepper together, then press the mixture into the mushrooms. Sandwich the mushrooms together in pairs. Thread the mushrooms and tomatoes on to 4 skewers. Mix the glaze ingredients together and brush over the mushrooms. Wrap the kebabs loosely in foil and cook on the barbecue or in the oven for about 5 minutes. Serve with the juices spooned over.

---

**30** kcals each

**2** g fat each

200g (1lb) closed cup mushrooms
**For the marinade:**
150g carton of natural Greek-style yoghurt
2 tablespoons chopped fresh mint
1 large garlic clove, chopped very finely
1 tablespoon paprika pepper
1 tablespoon lemon juice

## Minty Mushroom Kebabs

*Preparation and Cooking time: 4 hours marinating + 20 minutes*
*Makes 8 kebabs*

Soak 8 satay sticks if using instead of kebab sticks. Mix the marinade ingredients together in a large bowl. Add the mushrooms and stir until all are well coated. Cover and leave to marinate for at least 4 hours, stirring occasionally. Preheat the grill if using. Thread on to 8 kebab or satay sticks. Cook on a sheet of foil on the barbecue or under a moderate grill for about 5 minutes.

---

**80** kcals each

**5** g fat each

5 tablespoons grapeseed oil
3 tablespoons balsamic vinegar
3 garlic cloves, chopped finely
120g pack of shiitake mushrooms
12 brown/chestnut mushrooms
12 large closed cup mushrooms, halved

## Garlic Mushroom Kebabs

*Preparation and Cooking time: 2 hours marinating + 20 minutes*
*Makes 8 kebabs*

Mix the oil, vinegar and garlic together in a large bowl. Add the mushrooms and stir gently to thoroughly coat the mushrooms. Leave to marinate for at least 2 hours. Preheat the grill if using. Thread the mushrooms on to skewers. Cook on a barbecue or under a moderate grill for about 5 minutes, turning regularly, and brushing with any remaining marinade.

*Mushroom and Cheese Kebabs (left), Minty Mushroom Kebabs (centre), Garlic Mushroom Kebabs (right)*

8 large flat or portabello mushrooms
olive oil, for greasing
**For the filling:**
3 tablespoons oil
250g (9oz) lardons
1 small red chilli pepper, de-seeded and chopped finely
grated rind and juice of 1 lime
25g (1oz) fresh brioche crumbs or breadcrumbs
50g (2oz) sweetcorn kernels

## Chilli and Bacon Stuffed Mushrooms

*Preparation and Cooking time: 20 minutes · Makes 8*

If using the oven, preheat it to Gas 5/190°C/375°F. Heat 1 tablespoon of oil and cook the lardons and chilli pepper for 2 minutes. Transfer to a bowl with the remaining ingredients including the remaining 2 tablespoons of oil. Mix together thoroughly. Place the mushrooms on large squares of lightly oiled foil. Spoon the filling mixture on to each mushroom. Fold the foil to make loose parcels, sealing the edges together well. Cook on the barbecue or in the oven for about 10 minutes.

875g (2lbs) open cup mushrooms
25g (1oz) salt
1 teaspoon green peppercorns
1 teaspoon whole allspice
10 cloves
5cm (2-inch) piece of fresh root ginger, peeled and grated
450ml (16 fl oz) tarragon vinegar

## Mushroom Ketchup

*Preparation time: 15 minutes + overnight · Cooking time: 65 minutes*
*Makes about 1 litre (1¾ pints)*

Break the mushrooms into small pieces and put them into a large bowl. Sprinkle over the salt. Cover and leave overnight. The next day, drain off the salty liquid. Transfer the mushrooms to a stainless steel or enamel pan. Crush the peppercorns and allspice and add to the mushrooms with the grated ginger and vinegar. Bring to the boil and simmer, uncovered, for 30 minutes.

Cool, then liquidise until smooth. Pour into hot sterilised jars and seal. Place the jars in a deep saucepan with simmering water to the level of the neck of each jar. Keep the water at simmering point for 30 minutes. Remove the jars from the water. Cool. Check the seals are tight. Label and store in a cool place for at least a week before opening. It will last for about 3 months. Serve at barbecues or with brunch, light lunch and supper dishes.

**Tip:** A large cooked mushroom in a bap makes a splendid veggie burger.

*Chilli and Bacon Stuffed Mushrooms*